"True friendship's laws are
by this rule expressed,
Welcome the coming, speed
the parting guest."

—Alexander Pope

"A merry host makes
merry guests."

—Dutch Proverb

guest rooms

guest rooms

Hilary Héminway
& Alex Heminway

Photographs by Audrey Hall

Gibbs Smith, Publisher
Salt Lake City

First Edition
09 08 07 06 05 5 4 3 2 1

Published by
Gibbs Smith, Publisher
P.O. Box 667
Layton, Utah 84041

Orders: 1.800.748.5439
www.gibbs-smith.com

Designed by Dawn DeVries Sokol
Printed and bound in Hong Kong

Library of Congress Cataloging-in-Publication Data

Heminway, Hilary.
  Guest rooms / Hilary Heminway and Alex Heminway ; photographs by Audrey
Hall.—1st ed.
      p. cm.
  Includes bibliographical references.
  ISBN 1-58685-779-7
  1. Guest rooms. 2. Interior decoration. 3. Hospitality. I. Heminway, Alex. II. Title.

NK2117.B4H46 2005
395.3—dc22
                                        2005015413

To family, then and now—
generous hosts and (sometimes) good guests.

contents

"Could we have made it home again—and Zeus
give us no more hard roving!—if other men
had never fed us, given us lodging?"

—*Meneláos,* *The Odyssey*

"Austin's whole long boyhood had been full of visiting aunts and uncles and cousins
who came and stayed sometimes for a month or more. Lawyers, judges, politicians,
railroad men, business acquaintances, anybody that Judge King liked or was inter-
ested in or felt sorry for, he brought home from his office for a meal, for overnight,
and never thought of letting his wife know beforehand. The dining-room table
could be stretched out until it accommodated any number, and there was always
plenty of food. . . . Having company meant putting clean sheets on the bed in this
or that spare room and making up the couch in the billiard room so that some
young cousin, or sometimes Austin, could sleep on it, and then settling down to a
nice long visit."

—*William Maxwell,* *Time Will Darken It*

acknowledgments

We would like to thank the following people without whom this book would not have been possible: Gibbs Smith, Suzanne Taylor, and Aimee Stoddard for their kind direction; Audrey Hall for her photographs (and Chaco); and Tobin Heminway for her game assistance.

Untold thanks to all our generous friends who are exemplars of hosting: Susan and Roy O'Connor, Sophie and Derek Craighead, Bill and Robin Weiss, Joy and Jonathan Ingham, Dane Nichols, Tom and Diane Smith, Olga and Lyman Goff, Susan and George Matelich, John and Kathryn Heminway, Rodman Primack and Rudy Weissenberg, Robert Chan, Jay and Pauline Heminway, and Annabel and Clint Davis (for the loan of Perfect Persian Puss).

Thank you also to Kathy Niles, Jean Caswell, Harriet Vaughan, Sandy Johnston, Susan Gentile, Rhea Smart, Pat Brownlee, and Lark Polari for their hard work and friendship.

foreword

How can we give our guests just the right care and circumstance? Too little can leave them wondering whether or not they should have bothered coming. Too much can leave us wondering when they are finally going to leave.

"We were into things, but now we're into experiences."

Guests come in all sorts and for all sorts of reasons. They may be helpful and easy and go handsomely with our interior decoration and dinner parties. They may carry fresh and buzzing gossip. Some require more attention than others, but some may be worth the extra attention. Guests can be witty, intelligent, or believably and delightfully complimentary—or all three at once! Their sincere and knowing compliments stir our souls. They understand, admire, and even adore us. They agree with everything we say in such an enthusiastic and deeply felt way! How refreshing and pleasant. We love these varieties.

Of course, as even kings and queens discovered long ago, not all guests delight us. Guests may arrive because we owe them or because they are a means to some end. And there are, of course, the inevitable relatives (remember to put away the con-

> "The ornament of a house is the friends who frequent it."
> —*Ralph Waldo Emerson*, essayist and poet

tended heirlooms) we have to have over now and then because we have the same parents, grandparents, or rich uncle.

Inevitably, we wonder why on earth we invited the particular guests that are already stirring around downstairs. We must have liked them at one time and wanted to know them better. But now we know more than we wanted. Here they are—clinking, clanking, murmuring. We instantly vow never again to say, "You must come by," after bragging about our digs towards the end of a long cocktail party. We never expected to see them again, let alone in our home.

Nonetheless, we breathe deeply, strap on a hosting grin, and descend the stairs—only to discover they have cleaned up the place and taken wonderful pictures of their stay with us. They proceed to give very interesting details about the people who gave the cocktail party where we met them. Turns out he is having an affair with—but this is no place for that. How fascinating! Without guests like these in our guest rooms, we would never have known.

—*William Hamilton*, playwright and cartoonist

both host and guest

We're different people today than we were yesterday, not always better but farther in the field. The spouse we kissed this morning is not the spouse we kiss at night. The sister at lunch last week brings new rhythm to Friday dinner. How can we measure change in a friend? A shorter temper, a braver face? That dark cicatrix on the hand? Estranged cousin, college mate—the guest we knew before arrives, the sum of new numbers. He offers from his cup the distillate of intervening days: the year abroad in Rome, the failed affair with Kate. Here is the joy in guests: they carry inside their bags new news from the outside world.

Although dictionaries may belie it, friends by definition are host to one another and by extension are guests in each other's lives. Beyond this common parcel—house, earth—they share higher ground, a rare psychic space as certain as soil where companions in close proximity own a history, think together, walk for a moment in lockstep.

Every day we sit in borrowed furniture under borrowed roofs in the lee of borrowed lamps. But daily we welcome people into our spheres of attention, offer our time and energy. We are at once hosts and guests.

Hosting does not require lavish expression—home-sewn sachets, special menus, petits fours. Hospitality, generosity, and nurturing are gestures enough. Roof, chair, lamp—elementary gifts are the most welcome favors.

"When hospitality becomes an art, it loses its very soul."

—Sir Max Beerbohm, essayist

Thank you then for conversations, shared meals, the comfort and care afforded by friends, simple pleasures now met with the same enthusiasm we apprehended youth's puerile aspirations. If the hurdle between youth's chatter and the nuanced conversation of advancing age is the lesson of humility, consider the following: we are everywhere guests, no place more so than the ground beneath our feet. In the long exile from mother's womb, every room is strange and new.

arrivals

An open gate is the opposite of a closed one: unobstructed and welcoming.

A visitor's first impression of your house is often made from the sidewalk or stoop. A controlled but exuberant border of plants—boxwoods, azaleas, and a standard cedar—is a salutation in green.

Facing: Greet your guest outdoors in the driveway or garden. If they catch you in the kitchen, they'll feel like they're intruding.

first things
first

Weak from work and travel (travel, after all, is work), who among us is not impatient for good cheer and a pillow? What better sight than a welcome door ajar? At sea in cold water, we're relieved to reach a solid floe in the current. Food, shelter, and companionship are necessary tonics, however pleasant or painful today was. And the best noise at night is the human voice.

Show your guests to their bedrooms shortly after they arrive. Let them unpack, test the bed, and feel at home.

Greet your guests with warmth and spirit. Your welcome will set the tone for their entire visit. Body language is fundamental: meet them with open arms.

Hard-pressed and lost or upbeat and well, every guest is honored. The Greeks treated unknown travelers best. Thirty centuries ago in *The Odyssey*, Meneláos shouted, "Bring these men to be our guests: unhitch their team!" Consider these welcome words as shrift for a visitor's sins: "Happy you're here. Sit and rest."

We can't know others as we know ourselves; to that extent, every guest is a stranger "and all is strange to him," to borrow from Paul Claudel.

"That's the secret of entertaining. You make your guests feel welcome and at home. If you do that honestly, the rest takes care of itself."

—*Barbara Hall,* author

The air, the mattress, and the dynamic are new. Talk is stilted, cards close. Put your guests at ease with a glass and a plate (everybody eats, how can we not be friends?).

Freed from the street, the guest is free to bathe, talk, or sleep. Little treasures are a gift: glass of wine, flowers by the bed, time, and conversation. Leave for later hard questions and sotto voce demands. Good guests will know the limits of house and host. Make them feel they can stay forever, although they mustn't.

Turn on your night-lights. They'll remind new guests of youthful comforts: the way is lit; care and protection are nigh.

A clean room, freshly cut flowers, a stack of books—simple, inexpensive gestures mean the most. Guests expect little more than the comfort of friendship, a bed, and a meal. Everything else is extra.

Ready your rooms with lit lights and a candle on the nightstand; they're greater courtesies than they appear.

"Hospitality, *n.* The virtue which induces us to feed and lodge certain persons who are not in need of food and lodging."

—Ambrose Bierce, author

Give guests time and space to unpack bags, rest from travel, and freshen up (croquet can wait). A visit to family or friends, if not a vacation, is a retreat from daily life. Consider your guests may want to sit and catch their breath; a few hours, or days, without an agenda may be the perfect gift.

A cane-backed daybed from India, books, and an old portable Califone record player are simple pleasures in this California guesthouse.

Every house is a stage set and hosts are directors, but the production needn't have a big budget to be a success. Appeal to all your guest's senses in simple, straightforward ways: cut fresh flowers, dim the lights, fold a luxurious blanket at the foot of the bed, set out a tray of lemonade, stop the dog barking.

Guests are coming—hide the pills and other unmentionables.

Detailed directions, maps, and tokens for public transportation are thoughtful amenities for any guest who is afield in new territory.

first things first

☐ Offer guests detailed directions to your house ("take a right half a mile past the red barn, turn left at the prison . . ."). When possible, fax or e-mail a map of the area.

☐ Get ahead of yourself: buy blueberries for breakfast muffins, pod the peas, marinate the roast.

☐ Set the table this morning for tonight's dinner.

☐ Put out a bowl of fruit: cherries in May and June; strawberries, blackberries, and huckleberries in July and August; apples, pears, and Jack-Be-Little pumpkins in fall; citrus in winter; bananas year-round.

☐ Wash the sheets, sweep under the rug, restrain the dog.

guest bedroom

Overstuffed pillows and a thick duvet with an imposing wall of quarried stone as counterpoint make for a welcome and surprising environment in the guest bedroom.

Empty the bureau, clean off the desk—give your guests space to spread out. They'll feel welcome if allowed to unpack.

Facing: All houses, old and new, are host to unwanted guests: mice in the cellar and bugs, among others. A mosquito net in the guest room and a flyswatter are an honest approach to a real problem and will ensure invited guests don't fly for the door.

a home away from home

If the twenty-first-century hotel is a paragon of nowhereness—second only to airports as the ne plus ultra of non-places (also included on this list are public storage facilities, outlet malls, parking garages, cineplexes; nowhere, it seems, is everywhere)—then bare closets, yawning drawers, credenzas free of photos are its corollary, empty amenities that hold nothing, and the kempt bed, paramount among them, is like a naïf awaiting the messiness of experience.

The perfect guest room is clean and cared for. Books are close at hand and ample bedding is the keynote.

Empty shelves in a hotel represent everything

missing in that hotel: stories, love, and trouble.

But lived-in bedrooms have all that and more:

beach glass to remember Easter's walk, Durrell's

novels, a Shriner's fez bought at flea market, the

bed of our making. In short, private bedrooms

have distinction.

By the nature of the relationship—visitor in a

strange house—no guest (nor lover, one might

Water is the way of life. Leave a carafe of it by the bedside.

"Who has not wished that his host would come out frankly at the beginning of the visit and state, in no uncertain terms, the rules and preferences of the household in such matters as the breakfast hour? And who has not sounded out his guest to find out what he likes in the regulation of his diet and modus vivendi?"

—*Robert Benchley,* humorist

Keep on hand a selection of seasonal bed coverings and blankets: summer-weight waffle weave, wool, all-weather duvet, granny's old afghan.

add) can feel entirely at ease in someone else's bedroom. The possessions that give a room its personality and would seem to grant us access to its secrets—lacquered box, summer snapshot, coat left in a closet, the bed where we, too, will sleep—are the very things that keep us feeling distant from house and host; the bed, the box, the photo seem to say: *you're not the first one here.* Life is full of threats. And color. Most rooms have received guests before us. But we're present now to mingle with the freighted air and everything it holds. When this visit is over, we'll have a story to tell. We'll have held, however briefly, a little ground in each other's lives.

"Laugh and the world laughs with you,
snore and you sleep alone."

—Anthony Burgess, author, composer, and critic

Above all else the guest room should be clean and private with plenty of light and a window that opens. Fresh air and a quiet corner are essential.

A clutch of cedar hangers and two robes in the guest closet aren't requirements (you aren't, after all, running a hotel), but such gracious touches will help establish a memorable visit for your guests.

If your guests don't have allergies, cut flowers are a welcome
embellishment in the guest room. Arrange forsythia with daffodils in
spring; roses, peonies, and lavender in early summer; dahlias at
summer's end; and rose hips in fall. When the weather cools, gather
maple leaves and cut boughs of evergreen.

Double beds are a thing of the past (unless you
have space for two in a room), queen beds are
standard, and kings are indulgent. Single beds allow
for the most flexibility: couples keep close, adversaries
turn to respective walls.

Don't worry about putting couples in a room with single beds. They can hold hands across the divide. This arrangement will remind them of being teenagers when closer contact was forbidden.

Guests should show respect for the house where they are staying by picking up their clothes and making the bed. A host loves seeing guests, not necessarily their underwear.

how to make **a bed**

- ☐ Use a mattress cover to protect your mattress from incontinent guests.

- ☐ Use a flat sheet and hospital corners if bottom sheets are not fitted.

- ☐ Make sure the topside of the top sheet faces down. Leave sixteen inches of extra sheet at the head of the bed; this will fold back to form a decorative cuff.

- ☐ Use a seasonal blanket: cotton in summer, wool in winter.

- ☐ Add an old-fashioned blanket cover. Failing that, use an extra top sheet, a quilt, an afghan, or vintage lace.

- ☐ Turn back top sheet cuff and tuck all layers.

- ☐ Fold a duvet or extra blanket at the foot of the bed.

- ☐ Arrange pillows starting at the headboard and work out. Use cotton pillow protectors and cotton cases to cover sleeping pillows. Cover larger decorative pillows with shams. Boudoir pillows, baby pillows, or neck rolls are an added touch.

guest bathroom

The guest bathroom should feel like a room apart, a private place in a new house. If guests are allowed to briefly possess one room, let it be this one.

If your means are slim, guests can make due with an outside seat—no great inconvenience for the unpretentious, the perfect test for highfalutin visitors.

Facing: Necessities in a guest bathroom are few: clean towels, soap, toilet paper, toothpaste, shampoo, and a door that closes.

a requisite room

Anyone who has spent prolonged time without plumbing will agree the bathroom is the unsung center of the house. Less dramatic and less fun (but not always) than the bedroom with its complex politics and baroque desires, and less busy than the communal kitchen with its public displays, the bathroom is nonetheless a singular retreat. No other place offers such a measure of privacy (even sleep seems full of people).

Soap needn't be infused with essence of oat-
meal or triple milled in your kitchen sink the
day before guests arrive. Supermarket soap is
sufficient as long as it's fresh and clean.

The necessity of this little closet is beyond debate. Kitchen calls, bed beckons, but bathroom pulls. In our culture of coarse thinking, the bathroom seems a frank place for basic function. Yes and no. It's the seat of both elementary needs and fixations as complex as calculus.

Toilet, shower, sink, foaming bergamot soap—the modern bathroom is a marvel of convenience and a luxury more than two and a half billion people are without. Remember camping for a month when you were sixteen and be grateful. Soap, towel, toothpaste, comb—the necessary list is short. Add patience from the host and guests will feel at home.

Think of it as high style meets low: antibacterial towelettes are a creative solution in a formal bathroom without a sink.

Facing: A terry-cloth robe, monogrammed with le nom de la maison or nipped from the Carlyle Hotel, is not essential. But if found hanging on a hook, it will be used—and remembered.

candle hints

- ☐ Trim the candle wick to one-fourth-inch before lighting it to prevent smoking.

- ☐ Burn a candle for an hour for every inch of circumference for even reduction.

- ☐ Blow out a candle by holding your finger upright in front of the flame to prevent wax splatter.

- ☐ Blacken the wick of a brand new candle to make it look better.

- ☐ Don't place a burning candle near an open window, curtains, small fingers, or long tails.

Candles are among the most conventional amenities, but they add undeniable charm, warmth, and movement to any room, especially the bath.

Simple touches in the bathroom are luxurious touches:
lotion, bath oil, salts. But nothing is richer than fresh
soap, a new toothbrush, and a stack of clean towels.

How often do we forget cotton swabs in our own lives? Unexpected bathroom supplies (Q-tips, conditioner, body wash) translate as added care— the host is paying attention.

Everyone looks in the medicine cabinet, even Aunt
  Ethel and Pastor Phil. Remove anything untoward you'd
rather not share with guests. This is, however, a
  perfect opportunity for practical jokes: the rubber
    tarantula next to the Zoloft.

Most people visit the bathroom five or six times a day. If you're hosting, you'd better have a clean one for your guests. If you polish one corner of the house before their arrival, let it be this one.

If guests share a bathroom with you, sweep it clean, cap the toothpaste, and hide the prophylactics. Although you're unabashed, your guests may not be.

Prior to retiring to bed in a strange house, we're all familiar with the terror of discovering that we left our toothbrush at home. With that in mind, leave toothpaste and an extra toothbrush in the guest bathroom.

the essentials

- ☐ Fresh bar of soap
- ☐ Kleenex and toilet paper
- ☐ Stack of clean towels
- ☐ Feminine products for the fairer guest
- ☐ Shampoo and conditioner
- ☐ Toothpaste
- ☐ Hair dryer

the niceties

- ☐ Scented candles
- ☐ Body wash and lotion
- ☐ Room spray
- ☐ Bath oil and salts
- ☐ Wet wipes
- ☐ The Farmer's Almanac

the medicine cabinet

- ☐ Band-Aids
- ☐ Q-tips
- ☐ Antacids
- ☐ Aspirin or ibuprofen
- ☐ Homeopathic sleep aid
- ☐ Imodium A-D

amenities

What is it about cut flowers? Romance, yes. Color, certainly. They represent the outdoors brought inside (the dubious triumph of Man over nature). Regardless, cut flowers say someone is paying attention—to you. These dahlias bloom throughout late summer and early fall.

Amenities—soap, books, candles—are offerings from the heart as well as the hand.

Facing: Some people live and die in the false atmosphere of air-conditioning, so inefficient, loud, and easy. But the fan—portable, directional—hums with a simple task: to blow cool wind on a hot day.

a little forethought

Visits (to and from) are breaks in the continuity of our privacy, small trespasses, albeit welcome ones. Adjustments to schedule and routine are required of both host and guest: forgo the morning run, lay an extra plate, adjust your volume down while singing in the shower.

*What are the amenities in this room?
Extra pillows, comforter, chair, cleared
nightstands, and a stool for bags—all of
them straightforward, inexpensive, and
attainable.*

Amenities are embellishments, not necessities, but they are a memorable means of welcoming guests into your house and are the mark of a considerate host.

Like most breaks, visits require a little glue: extra towels, bedside books, a bowl of fruit. The carafe of water on the night-stand is an offer of welcome and a wel-come offer. Extra hangers in the closet may seem a trifle, but they encourage your guests to unpack, and, knocking together, promise there is a place for them. Unfold the luggage rack and empty a drawer. In doing so, you confer ownership for the night and dispel the chill that hangs in a borrowed room.

sheet specifics

☐ Thread count refers to the number of threads per square inch. High-thread-count sheets are soft, lustrous, and expensive, but not necessary. Sheets with a 250 to 350 thread count are sufficiently comfortable and durable.

☐ Sheets that are 100-percent cotton are best and can be found in a variety of counts: muslin (128-140), percale (180-200), Pima (200-400), and Egyptian cotton (200 and above).

☐ Linen sheets are the ultimate in summer bedding but require ironing. Silks and satins are too slippery. Flannel sheets are warmest in winter.

☐ Flowered, striped, or patterned sheets are not as tightly woven as plain colors and will wear out faster.

"Hospitality consists in a little fire, a little food,
and an immense quiet."

—*Ralph Waldo Emerson,* essayist and poet

*No guest can survive in a strange house without a basket of stones
and an outsize chaise.*

Books that address local concerns and history will add color and depth to the surrounding geography.

Anticipation is a crucial element of hosting.
If you know your guest loves birds, leave binoculars
and a field guide on the bedside table. Give an area map
to joggers and a list of antique shops to scavengers.

Pastels, brushes, and paper laid out suggestively will urge your guests to get in touch with their inner Picasso.

Guests will remember the simplest courtesies: a water carafe on the nightstand, an eye pillow, space in an open drawer. All are kind gifts that guests will appreciate after a long day of travel.

When thinking about amenities, focus on simple not ceremonial touches: add an embroidered pillow to the bed rather than chocolates.

Cards, dice, and puzzles are quiet pastimes for quiet moments after the party is over and the dinner cleared.

A good book found in a
guest room is a vacation
inside a vacation.

Kleenex, like so many other conveniences in life, is taken for granted: forgotten before the cold, longed for during hay fever.

simple luxuries

☐ Night-lights keep guests on target during midnight errands.

☐ Kleenex seems a simple suggestion, but it has unsung uses beyond the nose; you can dry your eyes or plug ears when the host is snoring.

☐ Scented candles, scented candles, so many scented candles—they're ubiquitous and indulgent, but they add undeniable charm to the plainest room.

☐ Eye pillows help shut out distractions for those who are unused to a foreign bed. Nonessential, yes, but appreciated nonetheless.

meals

Dining alfresco (place settings optional) is always out of the ordinary and will serve for a memorable meal, barring ant infestations and high wind.

An inventive display of place cards is a simple, inexpensive way to make guests feel welcome.

Facing: A meal is a sculpture in motion: the host fashions food, ornaments the table, and represents (through the act of cooking for others) the human need for nourishment and communion.

mealtime
rituals

Every day we live behind a bulwark of noise: solo ruminations, a couple's banter, the family chant. These sounds thrum out as from an ever-present instrument. When guests arrive, they breach and amplify; everyday drone becomes a vital tune. Breakfast, lunch, and dinner brighten with secrets, stories, a chorus of questions and demands: "Listen to this . . . You won't believe . . . Where have you been?"

The meal is the linchpin of any visit.
Whether it's formal dining, a picnic on the lawn,
or breakfast for the overnight guest, amity and
good cheer will radiate out like the spokes of a wheel.

Meals are a basis for talk, whether it's spirited debate among friendly rivals or the softer but no-less-animated confessions of a visiting paramour. Guest and host are face-to-face at the most fundamental rite of the day. Humbled by the naked act of eating, we're predisposed to be open with one another. We share an elementary need for love and for nourishment. Talk is easy and ought to flow like water.

A variety of ambient lighting—candles, lamps, and a burning log—add further fire to the blaze of company.

"The number of guests at dinner should not be less than the number of the Graces nor exceed that of the Muses, i.e., it should begin with three and stop at nine."

—Marcus Terentius Varro, scholar

Strike the triangle: call your guests to dinner with conviction. Your confidence and engagement will put them at ease throughout the meal.

A photo of your guest, pinched from an old album, makes for a surprising place setting; it's a warm and heart-felt gesture.

"Even today, well-brought-up English girls are taught by their mothers to boil all veggies for at least a month and a half, just in case one of the dinner guests turns up without teeth."

—Calvin Trillin, author

The cook should be organized; nothing is more inviting than a clean, well-mannered kitchen.

Squeeze six lemons in two liters of sparkling water. Add sugar to taste, a sprig of mint, and lemon zest (nasturtiums are edible).

Be creative. Don't limit meals to the kitchen or the dining room. Pack a portable feast: breakfast in the woods, lunch by the fire, dinner in bed.

The ultimate host should be prepared for a dizzying
list of contemporary eating constraints: vegan, gluten free,
lactose intolerant. Ask about preferences and accommodate
within reason. Don't, however, feel compelled to radically
change your own diet. If your guests eat only broccoli, ask
them to bring a head, and recipes to go with it.

Fresh fruit—by the bed, on the breakfast table, in the entry hall—is a simple, inexpensive offering, but always a meaningful one. What is a better gift than food?

The more spent dishes and glasses the better: the meal was rich and full of good cheer . . .

. . . but a conscientious guest shouldn't leave the kitchen without getting to the bottom of the mess.

The written name is a powerful invocation. It says, "You belong here, now."

mealtime courtesies

☐ Serve regional specialties to out-of-town guests: Atlantic shrimp to visitors from the Rockies, garden-grown okra to city kids. Yes, food travels, but meats, fish, and produce from the farmers market are always fresher.

☐ Experiment when cooking for guests. And don't be afraid of a failed menu.

☐ Send out for pizza if you're too exhausted to cook.

☐ Avoid scented candles on the dinner table.

Pull up a chair and everybody squeeze. A crowded table—within reason—is an intimate table.

children

Keep visiting kids in the attic, in your own children's former room, in a safe corner—anywhere they can play and shout from noon until night.

Now that every child owns a PlayStation, old-fangled games like checkers, tag, and jacks—physical games with human interaction—may become fashionable novelties.

Facing: Bunk beds are a smart solution to limited space and to the problem of encouraging kids into bed. They're compact and convivial, and, by alluding to the cramped quarters of a ship's cabin, they evoke the thrill of the high seas.

the children
of guests

Children, a blithe, unruly nation, are the best guests: they entertain other children; they break unwanted ceramics from the last century; they make rough music; they allow us, in the absence of our own sons and daughters, to play parents for the weekend; and, in breaking the ashtray and pulling the cat's tail, they serve as a reminder that for some of us (deficient no doubt), being chargeless isn't a forlorn state of affairs.

"Who is there whom bright and agreeable children do not attract to play and creep and prattle with them?"

—*Epictetus*, Stoic philosopher

Adulthood is navigation: abroad in our barks, we pilot the straits of relationships and, on occasion, run aground. Schooled as we are in armchair psychology, fear, anxiety, and insecurity are familiar if not always discussed symptoms of this or that neurosis. But in children, unedited emotion—dark and light—is on full display. "Now when I am old my teachers are the young," wrote Robert Frost at the age of fifty. How much easier our own crossings would be if we could speak as freely as children. Let them talk and play—children are the center, the periphery, and everything between.

Three single beds—in a Three Bears room—can accommodate any number of children: three large, six small, or a combination thereof.

Children feel safe in small spaces for an obvious reason. Give them books and cake in this under-stairs womb.

A hot-water bottle dressed in an agreeable bear suit will soothe any stomach strained by too much candy.

"In America, there are two classes of travel: first class, and with children."

—Robert Benchley, humorist

"All of us have moments in
our lives that test our courage.
Taking children into a house
with white carpet is one of them."

—*Erma Bombeck*, author and humorist

When left to their own devices, children will uncover endless entertainment in a strange house: great-grandfather's Fabergé egg, a beloved pashmina shawl, Puss the Cat. But isn't everything expendable in service to the happiness of youth?

Facing: Any room is easily converted into a children's bedroom with the quick addition of a stuffed bear.

Bicycles are an ideal diversion for the post-training wheels crowd. Be sure to remind them to mind the road.

Be vigilant when hosting kids and dogs. Tension and teeth may precede a period of détente.

A host should provide rules, toys, and activities for children of guests. Assign duties to guests' children to make them feel involved: have them pick dandelions and amuse the dog. Whenever possible, establish a separate play area for them in the den, attic, basement, backyard, or bedroom—anyplace safe and within earshot.

Kids are the focus of fixed attention.
When they accompany a guest, however,
they shouldn't be the focus of all the
attention. Guests should be mindful of their
host, who may have other interests besides
children and who may possess limited patience.

The ideal bedroom for children offers space to spread out and beds to hide under.

distractions for **children**

☐ Fresh air saves children! Unload them in the yard and turn on the hose and sprinkler.

☐ No need for kids to argue over video games when they have plenty of crayons and paper.

☐ Bubbles, for ages three and up: in a large bowl, stir together one part liquid dish soap, one part glycerin, and six parts water. Shape bubble blowers from wire.

☐ An empty pickle jar is great for catching and keeping bugs.

☐ Whipped cream is an ideal diversion but not in the living room.

Facing: If you have frequent family visits from nieces and nephews, or from friends with young children, keep dolls and teddy bears handy.

the unexpected guest

Crisis breeds creativity. Approach the sudden appearance of friends and enemies with humor and resourcefulness: give your bed to the former, the bed of your truck to the latter.

Almost any piece of furniture dressed with blankets, pillows, and cushions can serve as an improvised berth, whether it's a chaise, a sofa, or a barcalounger.

Facing: A vase of dahlias, an excess of pillows, and a cashmere blanket make this sheltered nook a desirable bed.

impromptu accommodations

Couch, quilt, towel—simple means will provision the unexpected guest. Who doesn't love terry-cloth robes, daiquiris by the pool, acupressure at ten? But one needn't deliver South Beach to the guest who calls from the corner. The sudden visitor may be on vacation, but his host isn't. Courtesy and restraint are required from the former, patience and generosity from the latter.

Where's the wine? Unexpected guests
are here: the prodigal son; the boss;
a new lover, an old lover; the over-served;
wayward teens; displaced neighbors;
runaway dogs. Treat them
all in kingly fashion.

Every host should expect the unexpected, but guests shouldn't expect if unexpected. Simple means will suffice—towel, tent, coffee from a can. And biscuits for the dog that surprises with his master.

The gracious guest, unexpected or otherwise, will accept any proffered accommodations with a game attitude: "Don't mind me, just happy to be here."

"Staying with people consists in your not having your own way, and their not having theirs."

—*Maarten Maartens,* author

Baby is secure in the bosom of sleep. This chest of drawers, family heirloom for a reason, furnishes a sturdy crib.

Facing: Stop the taps and pad the tub—no need for a bath before bed.

In a pinch, gather the bare essentials: pillow, blanket, and patience. A pullout couch and a privacy screen are all that are needed to create a guest space.

Extra amenities—Porthault linens, cashmere throw, a shot of bourbon—will assuage the distress of sleeping on linoleum.

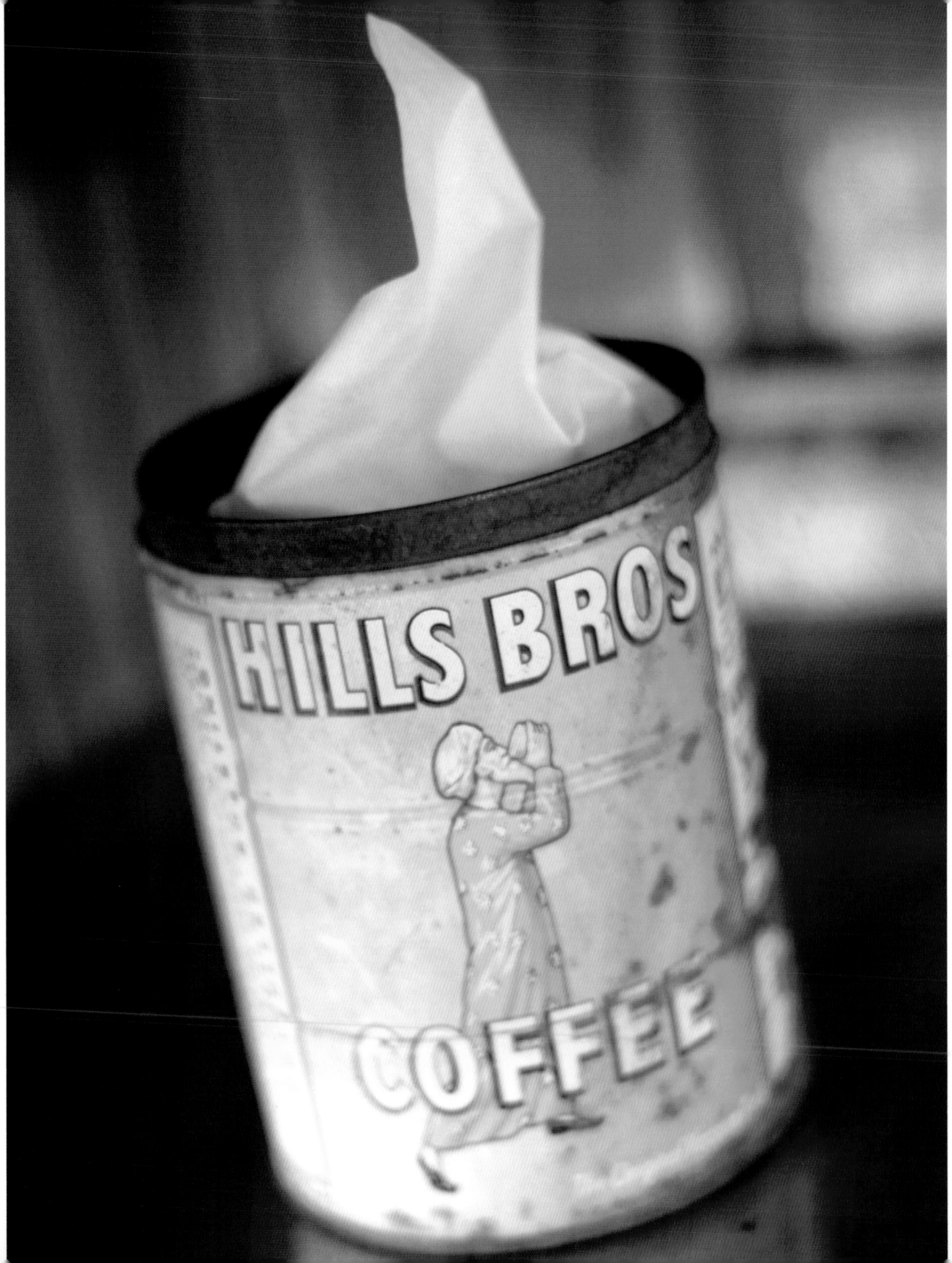
HILLS BROS
COFFEE

If unannounced visitors didn't have time to call ahead, chances are they didn't have time to blow their nose or clean their ears. Kleenex and Q-tips will right those wrongs.

Provision your home with the most basic necessities, and you'll be prepared for the unexpected. The pleasure of your company should be enough nourishment for the uninvited.

"To turn away a guest
is poorest poverty.
To bear with fools
is mightiest might."

— *Tiruvalluvar,* Indian sage

An outside shower is always an unexpected pleasure. We rarely leave our clothes behind and take the air without embarrassment.

beds for
unexpected guests

☐ Clear cushions from the couch.

☐ Fill up the air mattress. It's a perfect solution— cheap, comfortable, and easy to store in the closet.

☐ Hang a hammock from the oak, pitch a tent out back, dress the porch swing with pillows and blankets if the weather is nice.

☐ Put a bedroll in the bathtub (there are worse places to sleep).

A refrigerator, a reading lamp, and a canvas love seat convert this screened porch into suitable lodgings for anyone except your grandmother.

the good guest

A conscientious guest, ever mindful that visits are impositions regardless of a host's protestations to the contrary, will leave the guest room the way he or she found it: lights dimmed, sheets tucked, pillows straight.

Chairs are for sitting—the necessity of a guest room free of traveler's detritus (dirty laundry, scraps) is beyond debate. Keep your socks in your duffel.

Facing: Visits often correspond to vacations, and vacations connote rest: sleep late, lounge, read in bed—but don't keep your host waiting. A guest in bed past lunch is a laggard.

shared company

"*Good guest*" alliterates: two syllables jump forward in the mouth from guttural gates through a soft central sound of vowels to their palatal end. Through the front gate, the good guest is welcomed into the soft center of a house, lingers under roof, and, although he or she is not expelled at the end, leaves quickly, all departures being sudden. Alliteration here is an apt flourish; congruous syllables admonish: the good guest must be agreeable.

Like poker players, good guests should know
when to fold their cards and exit the game.

A visit is a collation of parallel narratives: *you and I live together in this place, now*. Guest and host are charged with the same duty: to correspond and to accommodate. Like two equidistant lines, they should allow each other a measure of space, physical and psychic. In due course, both will return to a separate course. Until then, they commit to a common transit. Both should be thankful for shared company along the way.

Make your bed—assume the day you wake up in a friend's house is the maid's day off.

Flexibility is the watchword for both guest and host. Go with the flow regardless of the other's lifestyle: night owls can read in their rooms if guests are early to bed, guests can walk the neighborhood if their host needs a few quiet hours alone. The good guest should be independent.

Like a breeze through an open window, the good guest brings fresh air into a closed house.

A considerate guest should be prepared to be flexible: sleep in the loft, sleep on the couch, or, when all cushions fail, accept with pleasure the bathtub, the floor, or the barn.

Consideration wins the day: use your own cell phone or a calling card; don't bring dirty laundry; wash dishes; take out the trash; be gracious. A handwritten thank-you note is required no matter how short the stay. Longer visits may call for a gift or for reciprocated hospitality.

A small parting gift and a thank-you note via post or handwritten on a significant stone is a gracious end to any visit.

the perfect house gift

- ☐ Grade-A maple syrup.

- ☐ Virgin olive oil.

- ☐ Black-oil sunflower seeds for your host's cardinals, sparrows, and chickadees; suet for nuthatches and woodpeckers.

- ☐ Dog biscuits.

- ☐ A packet of nasturtium seeds for the green thumb.

- ☐ Cheddar cheese and a mouse trap.

When considering a housewarming gift, the good guest will anticipate the passions of friends: bird feeders for bird-watchers, seeds for green thumbs.

departures

Consider her freckles and her almond eyes; remember the timbre of his voice. Breathe deeply and be awake—time together is brief.

Clocks are a mixed blessing: they tell time, but, with a sweep of hands, they remind us that all life is motion—present circumstances are ephemeral. Regardless, an alarm clock in the guest room is a sensible aid to sleep-bound visitors with trains to catch.

Facing: All visits are pregnant with an acute poignancy: everyone departs.

please
come again

Before the fluency of modern travel, hosting often meant adopting: fifty years ago, when conveyance was less kind, kinfolk from some distant ancestral precinct—sometimes the whole family—might materialize in the driveway, discharge their steamer trunk from the sedan, unleash a Pekinese in the tulips, and discommode the kitchen for the better part of a season.

A sweep of the house is recommended before departures to save paying postage for the tennis shoe left under the bed.

Today, hosting is less of a time commitment than it once was. Sometimes it's a summer, more often than not it's one week, weekend, or night. In other words, guests go. To be left behind in a house freshly painted by company is a melancholy conclusion. But many of us yearn to be alone. Here is one of life's ambiguities: we crave people, and we want to be delivered from them.

Visits long and short are lessons in humility, fraternity, and benefaction during which friendships bind but sometimes break. Connection isn't easy, sometimes it isn't the answer. Weather changes, as it should. Our time together—good and bad—is vapor spent, and like a wind-blown cloud in passing, passes.

Close the windows and pull the door shut as you leave. Be grateful for a friend's solid roof and last night's sound sleep.

What did we gain from this visit? The passing chance to live outside our own narrow routines.

Facing: Before leaving, turn and take a parting look at the declension of the hills and concede: we may never see this view again.

"I always feel that I have two duties to perform with a parting guest: one, to see that he doesn't forget anything that is his; the other, to see that he doesn't take anything that is mine."

—Alfred North Whitehead, philosopher

The simplest parting gift, be it pears or preserves, is more meaningful to your host than none at all.

Facing: Guest books are a repository of memories and thanks. In this age of digital dispatches and fewer handwritten letters, the guest book celebrates our script.

Make certain visitors leave a little of themselves behind as a reminder to you of the pleasures and perils of hosting; ask them to pose for a picture and sign the guest book. In return, give them a little gift to remember their stay: a book from the nightstand, a recipe, flowers from the garden, a sweater they admired.

159

how to get rid of
unwanted guests

- ☐ Flip the breaker switch.

- ☐ Give your hands a rest: let the dog lick dishes clean.

- ☐ Set rattraps in conspicuous corners.

- ☐ Feign death.

A long ramble, an anecdote from dinner, earnest thanks,
a Polaroid, a sketch—all are welcome in the guest book.

resources

ARCHITECTS

Emilio Ambasz
8 E. 62nd St.
New York, NY 10021
212.751.3517
www.ambasz.com
info@ambasz.com

Steve Dynia
135 Maple Ln.
Jackson, WY 83001
307.733.3766
sdynia@dynia.com

Goff Architecture
9 Popon Rd.
Watch Hill, RI 02891
401.348.9955

J. T. Foote & Associates
Paul Beryelli
140 E. Main St.
Bozeman, MT 59715
406.587.8888

Jeff Sheldon
PO Box 626
Lewistown, MT 59457
406.538.2201

Worcester & Worcester
(landscape architects)
40 Broad St.
Lyme, CT 06371
860.227.1143

CANDLES

Crafted Candles
800.635.0274
www.craftedcandles.com
info@craftedcandles.com

Illuminations
Stonestown Galleria
3251 - 20th Ave.
San Francisco, CA 94132
800.621.2998
www.illuminations.com
custserv@illuminations.com

Joya Candles
PO Box 230123
New York, NY 10023
718.852.6979
www.joyacandle.com
info@joyacandle.com

Northern
Lights Candles
3474 Andover Rd.
Wellsville, NY 14895
585.593.1200
www.northernlightscandles.com
info@northernlightscandles.com

Yankee Candle Store
PO Box 110
South Deerfield, MA 01373
800.243.1776
www.yankeecandle.com
info@yankeecandle.com

FARMERS MARKETS

Local Farmers Markets
(listed by state)
www.ams.usda.gov/farmersmarkets/
  map.htm
velma.lakins@usda.gov

HOSTESS GIFTS

Adirondack Reflections
PO Box 236
Keene, NY 12942
518.576.9549
www.adirondackreflections.com
info@adirondackreflections.com

Caroline's
888.801.2253
www.carolinescakes.com
caroline@carolinescakes.com

Cinnabar Creek
219 McLeod St.
Big Timber, MT 59011
406.932.5372
cinnabar@nmsn.net

Country Classic Gift Baskets
610.763.4993
www.countryclassicgiftbaskets.com
sales@countryclassicgiftbaskets.com

Epicurean Foods International
300 Mill St., #9
Kitchener, ON N2M 5G8 Canada
877.533.2636
www.epicureanfoods.com
info@epicureanfoods.com

Fortnum & Mason
5 Edgemoor Rd., Ste. 210
Wilmington, DE 19809
877.533.2636
www.fortnumandmason-usa.com
orders@fortnumandmason-usa.com

Fred Segal Beauty
420 Broadway
Santa Monica, CA 90401
888.644.5900
www.fredsegalbeauty.com

Harrods, Ltd.
87-135 Brompton Rd.
Knightsbridge
London, United Kingdom SW1X 7XL
020.7730.1234
www.harrods.com

Kensington Wine Market
1257 Kensington Rd. NW
Calgary, AB T2N 3P8 Canada
888.283.9004
www.kensingtonwinemarket.com
atyourservice@kensington
   winemarket.com

Manhattan Fruitier
105 E. 29th St.
New York, NY 10016
800.841.5718
www.manhattanfruitier.com

Nolechek's Meats, Inc.
PO Box 599
Thorp, WI 54771
800.454.5580
www.nolechekmeats.com
nolechek@nolechekmeats.com

RedEnvelope
PO Box 600040
San Diego, CA 92160
877.733.3683
www.redenvelope.com

See's Candies
20600 S. Alameda St.
Carson, CA 90810
800.347.7337
www.sees.com
qdordering@sees.com

Sunup Gallery
95 Watch Hill Rd.
Westerly, RI 02891
401.596.0800
www.sunupgallery.com

White Flower Farm
PO Box 50
Litchfield, CT 06759
800.503.9624
www.whiteflowerfarm.com
custserv@whiteflowerfarm.com

JOURNALS

A. T. Cross Co.
One Albion Rd.
Lincoln, RI 02865
800.282.7677 (Canada & USA)
www.cross.com
ecommerceord@cross.com

LIGHTING

Blanche Field
One Design Center Pl.
Boston, MA 02210
617.423.0715
www.blanchefield.com

Charleston Lighting &
  Manufacturing, Inc.
212 E. I-65 Service Rd. N
Mobile, AL 36607
800.661.9224
www.charlestonlighting.com
sales@charlestonlighting.com

Distinctive Lighting
2608 W. Main St.
Bozeman, MT 59718
800.995.7172
www.distinctivelighting.com

Hubbardton Forge
PO Box 827
Castleton, VT 05735
802.468.3090
www.vtforge.com
info@vtforge.com

Klaff's
28 Washington St.
South Norwalk, CT 06854
800.552.3371
www.klaffs.com

Murray Feiss Lighting
125 Rose Feiss Blvd.
Bronx, NY 10454
718.292.2024
www.feiss.com
sales@feiss.com

Restoration Hardware
15 Koch Rd., Ste. J
Corte Madera, CA 94925
800.910.9836
www.restorationhardware.com
webcs@restorationhardware.com

Rocky Mountain Design
601 W. Park St.
Livingston, MT 59047
800.648.0162
www.rockymountaindesign.com
rmdi@rockymountaindesign.com

Shades of Light
4924 W. Broad St.
Richmond, VA 23230
800.262.6612
www.shadesoflight.com
visitor@shades-of-light.com

LINENS

Bed Bath & Beyond
410 E. 61st St.
New York, NY 10021
800.462.3966
www.bedbathandbeyond.com

The Company Store
500 Company Store Rd.
La Crosse, WI 54601
800.285.3696
www.thecompanystore.com
custserv@thecompanystore.com

The Crossroads
27 E. Main St.
Bozeman, MT 59715
406.587.2702
gallery@earthlink.com

D'Porthault Linens
18 E. 69th St.
New York, NY 10021
212.688.1660

Frette
799 Madison Ave., #1
New York, NY 10021
212.988.5221
www.frette.com

Garnet Hill
800.870.3513
www.garnethill.com
japandivision@garnethill.com

Heirloom Linens
#380 - 777 Royal Oak Dr.
Victoria, BC V8X 4V1 Canada
800.292.7171
www.heirloomlinens.com
info@heirloomlinens.com

Horchow Collection
Neiman Marcus Stores
877.944.9888
www.horchow.com

L. L. Bean, Inc.
Freeport, ME 04033
800.441.5713 (Canada & USA)
www.llbean.com

Linen Press
49 W. Main St.
Mystic, CT 06335
860.536.5192

Pottery Barn
59th & Lexington
127 E. 59th St.
New York, NY 10022
888.779.5176
www.potterybarn.com

Williams Sonoma
Eaton Centre
220 Yonge St.
Toronto, ON M5B 2H1 Canada
416.260.1255
www.williams-sonoma.com

Williams Sonoma
3250 Van Ness Ave.
San Francisco, CA 94109
877.812.6235
www.williams-sonoma.com

MATTRESSES

The Mattress Co.
3120 N. 27th Ave., #5
Phoenix, AZ 85017
888.773.7326
www.the-mattress-co.com
sleep-in-comfort@mattresses.net

Mattress Mill
8383 Huffine Ln.
Bozeman, MT 59718
406.586.4525

Royal Pedic
341 N. Robertson Blvd.
Beverly Hills, CA 90211
800.487.6925
www.royal-pedic.com
tk-royal@pacbell.net

SleepCountry
8 King St. E.
Toronto, ON M5C 1B5 Canada
888.753.3788
www.sleepcountry.ca

MEDICINE CABINET SUPPLIES

Boyd's
655 Madison Ave. (& 60th St.)
New York, NY 10021
800.683.2693
www.boydsnyc.com

CanadaPharmacy.com
800.891.0844
www.canadapharmacy.com

DrugStore.com
411 - 108th Ave. NE, Ste. 1400
Bellevue, WA 98004
800.378.4786
www.drugstore.com
aboutorders@drugstore.com

J. Leon Lascoff & Son
1209 Lexington Ave.
New York, NY 10128
212.288.9500

Watkins, Inc.
277 Hutchings St.
Winnipeg, MB R2X 2R4 Canada
204.477.0022
www.watkinsonline.com

Watkins, Inc.
150 Liberty St.
PO Box 5570
Winona, MN 55987
507.457.3300
www.watkinsonline.com

MUSIC

Amoeba Music
510.549.1125 Berkeley, CA
415.831.1200 San Francisco, CA
323.245.6400 Hollywood, CA
www.amoebamusic.com

Cactus Records
29 W. Main St.
Bozeman, MT 59715
406.587.0245

Newbury Comics
www.newburycomics.com
retaillocations@newburycomics.com

Musiquest
63E Donnegani
Pte. Claire, QC H9R 2V9 Canada
514.426.0876

Other Music
15 E. 4th St.
New York, NY 10003
212.477.8150
www.othermusic.com

Rocks In Your Head
157 Prince St.
New York, NY 10012
212.475.6729
www.rocksinyourhead.com

SOAPS & BATH OILS

American Homestead Mercantile Co.
PO Box 1354
Bonsall, CA 92003
877.581.8101
www.ahmercantile.com

Bon Savon
13351-d Riverside Dr., #501
Sherman Oaks, CA 91423
877.832.4635
www.bonsavon.com
customerservice@bonsavon.com

Caswell and Massey, Ltd.
PO Box 6161
121 Fieldcrest Ave.
Edison, NJ 08818
800.326.0500
www.caswellmassey.com

Crabtree and Evelyn
55 Avenue Rd.
Toronto, ON M5R 3L2 Canada
416.929.0109
www.crabtreetoronto.com
info@crabtreetoronto.com

Crabtree and Evelyn
PO Box 167
Woodstock, CT 06281-0167
800.272.2873
www.crabtree-evelyn.com

Floris
703 Madison Ave.
New York, NY 10021
800.535.6747
www.florislondon.com

L'Occitane En Provence
510 Madison Ave.
New York, NY 10022
888.623.2880
usa.loccitane.com

Roger-Gallet
YSL BEAUTE Canada, Inc.
2830 Argentia Rd., Ste. #1
Mississauga, ON L5N 8G4 Canada
905.542.46.60

Roger-Gallet
YSL BEAUTE, Inc.
Gucci Tower
685 - 5th Ave., 10th Fl.
New York, NY 10022
212.715.7333
www.roger-gallet.com
roger-gallet.usretail@us.yslbeaute.com

Waterworks
800.927.2120
www.waterworks.com

Zitomer
969 Madison Ave.
New York, NY 10021
888.217.8222
www.zitomer.com
info@zitomer.com